A TREASURY OF CLASSIC POULTRY RECIPES

by
Michelle A. Preston

TABLE OF CONTENTS

INTRODUCTION

With *A Treasury Of Classic Poultry Recipes*, Michelle A. Preston has created a collection of diverse dining delights from the world of game and fowl. Chicken, turkey, duck, goose, squab, pigeon, quail, pheasant . . . no matter what bird you are in the mood for, you'll surely find dozens of delicious recipes that will satisfy both you and your family.

The bulk of the book consists of chicken and turkey recipes. Chicken has always been one of America's favorite foods. It's both economical and nutritious, and the variety of ways you can cook chicken is virtually endless. Turkey, while mainly thought of as a holiday dish, is actually a popular food served all year round. Like chicken, it is very cost efficient and full of nutrients, and there are a number of creative ways to cook the bird.

The remainder of the book is filled with fabulous recipes for specialty birds and game. And you don't have to be a hunter to enjoy these fine foods! They are all readily available at various supermarkets, butchers, and specialty food stores across the country. While some people are unfamiliar with these more "exotic" dishes, any hesitation is soon washed away with the first bite of a mouth-watering recipe that utilizes one of these luscious birds.

Whether you're eating poultry because it's good for you or just because you enjoy its subtle taste, and whether you're frying, roasting, baking or simmering, with *A Treasury Of Classic Poultry Recipes*, Michelle A. Preston guarantees that you'll find a recipe that will meet your culinary requirements. Experiment and enjoy!

CHICKEN

Chicken with Peaches

1 3-pound broiler, cut into serving sized pieces
1 can peach halves, drained
heavy syrup from peaches, heated
1 tablespoon onion, chopped fine
1 tablespoon soy sauce
¼ cup butter
1 teaspoon all-purpose

1) Add the soy sauce, onion, seasoning, and butter together. Coat each piece of chicken with the mixture. Place the chicken in an oven at 375 degrees for 1½ hours, basting constantly.

2) Place the peach halves, hole side up, around the chicken. Cook an additional 10 minutes.

Serves 4

Chicken Casserole

2 3-pound broilers, cut up into
serving sized pieces
3 cups water
1½ cup raw rice
2 small onions, chopped
2 stalks celery
dash of salt
6 eggs, beaten
2 cups milk
3 cups celery, chopped
1 teaspoon dried onion
1 teaspoon parsley
dash of pepper

1) Place the chicken in water with rice, onions, celery, and a dash of salt. Bring to boil, cover, lower flame, and simmer for 45 minutes. Remove chicken and let cool.

2) Strain the broth, remove the chicken meat from bones, and mix the chicken, the broth and the remaining ingredients together. Place in a casserole dish and bake at 350 degrees for 45 minutes.

Serves 6

Chicken in Sherry

8 chicken breasts
flour
salt and pepper to taste
2 (10¾ ounce) cans of chicken soup
1 8-ounce carton sour cream
1 4-ounce can mushroom pieces, drained
½ cup sherry
paprika
cooked rice

1) Debone chicken breasts and remove skin. Dust in mixture of flour, salt, pepper, and paprika. Brown in skillet in small amount of cooking oil.

2) Place chicken in a casserole dish. Melt butter and stir in soup, sour cream, mushrooms and sherry. Continue stirring and cook slowly until mixture is smooth. Pour over chicken. Cover and bake at 350 degrees for 1½ hours. Serve over rice.

Serves 8

Mrs. Katie S. Bradford
Jonesboro, LA

Basic Fried Chicken

3 2-pound fryers, cut into serving sized pieces
6 tablespoons butter or margarine
½ teaspoon salt
½ teaspoon pepper
1½ teaspoons all-purpose seasoning

1) Place the pieces of chicken in melted butter and fry until lightly brown. Sprinkle the seasoning, salt, and pepper. Cover the pan. Cook over low flame for 20 minutes, turning often.

2) Remove cover and cook for an additional 10 minutes, turning once.

Serves 6

Chicken with Blue Cheese

4 boneless chicken breasts
2 eggs, beaten
2 cups bread crumbs, crumbled
1 cup flour
1 pound blue cheese, crumbled
2 pints sour cream
8 cloves of garlic, pressed
2 tablespoons butter
2 tablespoons oil

1) Mix the eggs and bread crumbs together. Coat the chicken in flour and roll in the egg and bread crumb mixture.

2) Brown the chicken in oil and butter. Place browned chicken in a baking dish and set aside.

3) Mix the blue cheese, sour cream and the garlic. Pour the mixture over the chicken, cover, and place in a 350 degree oven for 45 minutes.

Serves 4

Green Apple Chicken

2 3-pound chickens, quartered
flour
4 tablespoons butter
6 green apples, pared, cored, and sliced
1½ teaspoons lemon juice
1½ cups chicken stock

1) Coat the chicken in flour. Lightly season with the salt and pepper. Place in melted butter and cook until brown. Place the slices of apple around the chicken, and pour the lemon juice and then the chicken stock over the top. Cover and simmer over a low flame for 45 minutes.

Serves 6

Lemon Chicken with Cinnamon

2 3-pound frying chickens, quartered
⅓ cup lemon juice
¾ teaspoon cinnamon
4 tablespoons olive oil
1½ teaspoons oregano
¾ teaspoon salt
¾ teaspoon pepper

1) Mix the lemon juice, cinnamon, oil, oregano, salt, and pepper together. Place the chicken in the sauce, and let marinate for 45 minutes, turning often.

2) Broil marinated chicken for 30 minutes, basting as you cook, and turning the chicken once.

Serves 6

Chicken, Wine and Grapes

3 pound broiler, cut into serving sized pieces
dash teaspoon salt
2 tablespoons butter
⅓ cup water
¾ cup white wine
dash of cloves
dash of rosemary
¾ cup seedless grapes

1) Lightly season the chicken with salt. Place seasoned chicken in butter and brown. Add the wine and the water.

2) Pour mixture into a casserole dish, add the cloves and rosemary, and place in an oven at 350 degrees for 30 minutes. Add the grapes and cook for an additional 20 minutes.

Serves 4

Chicken Pot Pie

1 whole "canned" chicken, skinned and boned
2 or 3 large potatoes, diced large
2 cups sweet peas (frozen)
1 can pimentos, chopped
1 large onion, chopped
⅓ stick butter or margarine
½ teaspoon each black pepper and paprika
salt to taste

1) Add broth and enough water to cover chicken. Salt to taste. Bring all ingredients to a boil in large dutch oven.

2) Add 1 can of biscuits, cut in ¼ inch pieces, mash under broth. Bake till brown at 450 degrees. Enjoy.

Serves 4

Mrs. A. B. Evans
Safford, AZ

Fried Garlic Chicken

2 2-pound fryers or broilers, cut into
serving sized pieces
3 cloves of garlic, minced
½ teaspoon all-purpose seasoning
½ cup milk
2 eggs, beaten
¾ cup flour
½ teaspoon garlic powder
½ teaspoon salt
¼ teaspoon pepper
2 cups fine bread crumbs
vegetable oil

1) Mix the garlic, seasoning, and milk together.
Add the eggs.

2) Coat the chicken in the flour.

3) Mix the garlic powder, salt, pepper and bread
crumbs together. Dip the pieces of chicken into the
milk and then roll in the bread crumbs. Fry in boil
oil until browned.

4) Place the browned chicken in a 350 degree
oven for 25 minutes.

Serves 4

Southern Fried Chicken

4 3-pound fryers, cut into serving sized pieces
4 cups milk
2 cups flour
2 teaspoons salt
1 teaspoon pepper
6 eggs, beaten
2 cups cracker meal
fat

1) Place the chicken in the milk for 1 hour. Shake the soaked chicken in a bag containing a mixture of flour, salt and pepper.

2) Combine the eggs with 1½ cups of the dry mixture, coat the chicken with it, and then roll in the cracker meal. Fry in hot fat for 25 minutes, turning often.

Serves 12

Chicken Tarragon

2 3-pound chickens, cut up into serving sized pieces
pinch of salt
pinch of pepper
4 tablespoons butter, melted
⅔ cup fresh tarragon, chopped
1 cup white wine

1) Lightly season the chicken with the salt and pepper. Place seasoned chicken in melted butter and cook until brown, adding tarragon as you cook.

2) Lower the flame, add the wine, cover, and cook for 45 minutes.

Serves 8

Italian Chicken

1 3-pound broiler, cut up into serving sized pieces
3 tablespoons butter, melted
2 cloves garlic, minced
¾ cup onions, chopped
¾ cup green pepper, chopped
¾ cup tomato sauce
1 can of tomatoes
¾ cup red wine
2 bay leaves
½ teaspoon thyme, crushed
½ teaspoon salt
¼ teaspoon pepper

1) Place the pieces of chicken in the melted butter and cook until brown.

2) Mix in the garlic, onions, green pepper, tomato sauce, and tomatoes. Add the wine, bay leaves, thyme, salt and pepper. Cover and cook over a low flame for 30 minutes, turning once.

Serves 4

Herb Chicken

2 3-pound frying chickens, quartered
¾ teaspoon thyme
¾ teaspoon sage
1½ teaspoons tarragon
4 tablespoons onion, minced
3 tablespoons butter
2 teaspoons lemon peel, grated
¼ teaspoon salt
½ teaspoon pepper
⅓ cup white wine

1) Mix the thyme, sage, tarragon, onions, butter, lemon peel, salt, and pepper together.

2) Cut small slices into the chicken, and place the butter mixture into the slits. Reserve ¼ of the mixture.

3) Melt the remaining butter mixture and stir in the wine.

4) Broil the chicken for 30 minutes, basting often with the wine mixture and turning once.

Serves 6

Roasted Chicken with Vegetables

3 pound broiler fryer
4 small potatoes, halved
3 carrots, cut diagonally
2 celery stalks, cut diagonally
2 onions, halved
1 small green pepper, sliced
10 ounces canned tomatoes
dash of salt
dash of pepper
1 tablespoon butter, melted
dash of paprika

1) Place the chicken and vegetables, with the exception of the tomatoes, on a large piece of foil in a roasting pan. Pour the can of tomatoes over the chicken and vegetables, and lightly season with salt and pepper. Loosely wrap the foil around the chicken, securing edges to keep the moisture inside.

2) Roast at 375 degrees for 1 hour. Remove foil, baste with pan juices, brush with butter, and sprinkle with paprika. Roast for an additional 20 minutes.

Serves 4

Pineapple Chicken (Hawaiian)

1 whole chicken, chopped into bite sizes
1 can Dole pineapple chunks
3 stalks green onions
3 tablespoons oyster sauce
2 tablespoons Aloha Shoyu
2 cloves garlic, smashed
1 finger of root ginger, smashed
salt to taste

1) Brown chicken in pan with oil, ginger and garlic. Add oyster sauce and shoyu, let simmer. Pour pineapple juice over chicken and simmer 15 minutes. Put in platter evenly.

2) Finely chop green onions and sprinkle over chicken. Garnish entire chicken with pineapple chunks.

Serves 4

Leon B. Wilson
Wahiawa, HI

Brandied Chicken

1 4-pound roasting chicken, cut into serving sized pieces
¼ teaspoon salt
¼ teaspoon pepper
4 tablespoons butter, melted
¼ cup onion, chopped
½ cup brandy
⅓ cup crem

1) Lightly season the chicken with the salt and pepper. Place seasoned chicken in melted butter and cook over a medium flame until brown.

2) Add the onion and continue to cook until it turns transparent. Add the brandy and mix until chicken is well-coated.

3) Cover the pan with aluminum foil, place in an oven, and cook at 350 degrees for 30 minutes.

4) Remove the foil, pour the cream over the chicken and cook for an additional 5 minutes.

Serves 4

Chicken with Rosemary and Sour Cream

2 3-pound chickens, cut up into serving sized pieces
½ teaspoon rosemary
dash of salt
dash of pepper
1½ cups chicken stock
1½ cups sour cream

1) Lightly season the pieces of chicken with rosemary, salt, and pepper.

2) Mix the sour cream and chicken stock together and pour it over the chicken.

3) Bake the chicken in a 300 degree oven for 1¼ hours.

Serves 6

Chicken Stuffed with Spinach and Bacon

2 chicken breasts, skinned, boned, and halved
4 slices bacon
1 small onion, chopped
6 ounces frozen spinach, thawed and chopped
1 egg, beaten
¼ cup croutons, crushed
¼ teaspoon garlic salt
1 tablespoon oil

1) Fry the bacon until crisp and remove, reserving 1 tablespoon of drippings. Add the onion to the drippings and cook until soft. Remove the pan from the flame and stir in the bacon, spinach, egg, croutons, and garlic salt.

2) Slice a pocket into each halved chicken breast, and stuff with the spinach and bacon mixture. Fasten with toothpicks.

3) Cook chicken in hot oil for 15 minutes turning once.

Serves 4

Fried Chicken with Gravy

3 pound fryer, cut up into serving sized pieces
½ cup flour
1 teaspoon salt
1 teaspoon pepper
⅓ cup butter
⅓ cup shortening
1½ cups half and half

1) Shake the chicken in a bag with ¼ cup flour, ½ teaspoon salt, and ½ teaspoon pepper. Mix the shortening and butter together. Brown the coated chicken over a high flame in the mixture. Lower heat, cover, and cook for 20 minutes. Remove cover and cook for an additional 10 minutes.

2) Remove the chicken, drain, reserving 2 tablespoons of fat, and blend in the remaining flour, salt, and pepper. Gradually stir in the half-and-half. Cook until rich and creamy, stirring often. Pour over chicken and serve.

Serves 4

Chicken Chow Bake

2 cups diced cooked or canned chicken
1 can cream of mushroom soup
1 9-ounce can (1 cup) pineapple tidbits
1 can cream of celery soup
½ soup can water
2 tablespoons soy sauce
1 cup celery slices
2 tablespoons chopped green onions
1 3-ounce can (2½ cups) chow mein noodles

1) Combine all ingredients except noodles, mixing well. Gently fold in 1 cup of the noodles.

2) Turn into 8 x 8 x 2 inch baking dish. Sprinkle with remaining noodles. Bake at 350 degrees for 50 minutes or until hot.

Serves 4

Sandra Peer
Hillsboro, OR

Roasted Chicken and Ham

**2 4-pound roasting chickens, cut in
half lengthwise**
⅓ cup butter, melted
2 cups lean ham, cubed
2 cups onions
2 cups mushrooms
1 teaspoon salt
1 teaspoon pepper
2 cups white wine

1) Brush the chicken with butter and place under a broiler until brown. Then turn the oven down to 350 degrees.

2) Place the ham, onions, and mushrooms around the chicken. Lightly season with the salt and pepper. Add the wine, cover with aluminum foil and place in a pre-heated 350 degree oven for 1 hour.

3) Remove the foil and cook for an additional 5 minutes.

Serves 6

Chicken on Fire

2 3-pound chickens
2 tablespoons butter
3 cloves garlic, minced
1½ cup bottled chili sauce
1½ teaspoon paprika
Juice of 1 lemon

1) Roast the chicken in a 350 degree oven for one hour.

2) Saute the garlic in the butter for 5 minutes. Stir in the remaining ingredients. Cook over a low flame for an additional 5 minutes. Stir continuously.

3) Carve the roasted chicken into serving sized pieces, place in a casserole dish, pour the garlic sauce over it, and heat over a medium flame for 3 minutes.

Serves 6

Sweet and Sour Chicken

2 3-pound frying chickens, cut into serving sized pieces
½ cup honey
2 teaspoons Dijon mustard
¾ teaspoon curry powder
¾ teaspoon ground ginger
⅓ cup lemon juice
3 teaspoons lemon peel, grated
3 teaspoons orange peel, grated

1) Mix the honey, mustard, curry powder, ginger, lemon juice, lemon peel, and orange peel together. Brush the mixture over the chicken, reserving half of the sauce.

2) Place the chicken in a 375 degree oven for 30 minutes, basting often with the pan juices. Turn the chicken over, brush with the remaining mixture, and bake for an additional 30 more minutes. Continue to baste often.

Serves 6

Herb Chicken in White Wine

3 pound broiler, quartered
½ teaspoon salt
¼ teaspoon pepper
⅓ cup butter
1 small onion, minced
¾ teaspoon tarragon
¾ teaspoon rosemary
¾ tablespoon parsley, minced
¾ tablespoon chives, minced
⅓ cup white wine

1) Lightly season the chicken with salt and pepper and saute in butter.

2) Add the onion and continue to saute for 10 minutes. Stir in the herbs, add the wine, and simmer over low flame, covered, for 25 minutes.

Serves 4

Chicken Enchiladas

1 fryer chicken, simmered, skinned, boned and sliced
3 cans cream of chicken soup
1 pint sour cream (if you don't like that much use ½ pint)
1 can diced green chilis (if you like it hot add 2)
½ cup oil
18 corn tortillas
3 cups shredded cheddar cheese
½ bunch green onions, chopped

1) Mix soup, sour cream and chilis in saucepan, cook until boiling. Heat oil in saucepan. Heat tortillas in oil till soft, drain on paper towel.

2) Put one heaping tablespoon of chicken mixture on each tortilla. Place in baking pan and pour rest of mix over top. Put cheese on top. Bake at 350 degrees for 30 minutes.

Serves 4

Mrs. Lewis Schnider
Cottonwood, ID

Fried Chicken with Paprika

3 2-pound fryers, cut into serving sized pieces
1½ teaspoon paprika
1 cup all-purpose flour
¾ cup corn meal
½ teaspoon salt
½ teaspoon pepper
½ cup butter, melted

1) Mix the paprika, flour, corn meal, salt, and pepper together. Coat the pieces of chicken with the seasonings.

2) Place the melted butter in a baking dish. Put the chicken in on top of the butter and place in a 350 degree oven for 1¼ hours turning often.

Serves 6

Indian Chicken

2 3-pound chickens, cut into serving sized pieces
4 tablespoons butter, melted
3 cloves garlic, minced
3 onions, chopped
1½ tablespoon almonds, ground
2 tablespoons curry powder
¾ teaspoon ginger
dash of salt
dash of pepper
1½ cup buttermilk

1) Saute the garlic and onions in the butter. Add the almonds, curry powder, ginger, salt, and pepper. Mix well.

2) Add the pieces of chicken, pour the buttermilk over the top, and simmer over a low flame for 45 minutes, turning the chicken once.

Serves 6

Garlic Chicken

2 3-pound frying chickens, quartered
3 garlic cloves, minced
¾ cup olive oil
3 tablespoons lemon juice
1½ teaspoons parsley, chopped
3 teaspoons rosemary
¼ teaspoon pepper

1) Mix the garlic, oil, lemon juice, parsley, rosemary, and pepper together. Coat the chicken with the sauce, cover, refrigerate for 6 hours, turning occasionally.

2) Barbecue the chicken for 45 minutes, turning and basting often.

Serves 6

Chicken, Macaroni and Cheese

¾ pound broiler chicken, cut into serving sized pieces
⅓ cup onion, chopped
½ tablespoon butter
8 ounces canned cream of chicken soup
1 cup cheddar cheese, shredded
½ cup chicken broth
2 small tomatoes, quartered
2 hard boiled eggs, chopped
6 ounces macaroni, cooked

1) Saute the onion in butter for 5 minutes. Add the soup and ¾ cup cheese, and continue to cook until the cheese melts.

2) Add the pieces of chicken, chicken broth, tomatoes, eggs, and macaroni to the soup. Mix well.

3) Pour into an oiled casserole dish, top with remaining cheese, and place in a 350 degree oven for 30 minutes.

Serves 4

Cornish Hen Acapulco

4 Cornish game hens

Baste:
¼ cup dry sherry
¼ cup salad oil
2 tablespoons soy sauce

Stuffing:
½ cup uncooked rice
2 tablespoons butter
1¼ cup hot chicken broth
1 egg, beaten
¼ cup chopped ripe olives
¼ cup chopped ripe olives
¼ cup slivered almonds
2 tablespoons fine dry bread crumbs
salt and pepper to taste

1) Mix ingredients for baste and set aside. Saute rice in butter until golden brown. Add broth and cover, simmer 20 minutes.

2) Stir in remaining ingredients—makes 2 cups, enough for 4 hens. Stuff each hen with ½ cup of the mixture. Follow package directions for roasting. Baste often until done.

Serves 4

Inge Bettenhausen
San Francisco, CA

Basic Barbecued Chicken

2 3-pound broilers, cut in half lengthwise
1¼ cup mayonnaise
3 tablespoons onion, chopped
1½ teaspoon paprika
½ teaspoon pepper
½ teaspoon salt
3 tablespoons honey

1) Mix all of the ingredients together with the exception of the chicken. Let stand for 30 minutes. Coat the inside and outside of the chicken with the mixture.

2) Place the chicken with the skin side down on the barbecue. Cook for 25 minutes, turn over, and cook for an additional 30 minutes. Baste continually during cooking.

Serves 6

Chicken and Mushroom Rolls

4 boneless chicken breasts, skinned, halved, and flattened
½ cup butter
4 tablespoons mushrooms, chopped
dash of salt
dash of pepper
1 egg, beaten
bread crumbs

1) Lightly dot the chicken breasts with butter, saving enough butter for frying later. Season with the salt and pepper and pour the mushrooms over the top. Roll up the breasts. Chill.

2) Place chilled chicken breasts in the egg and roll in the bread crumbs. Fry in remaining butter for 5 minutes.

Serves 8

Kung Pao Chicken

4 chicken breasts, skinned, boned, and halved
6 tablespoons soy sauce
6 tablespoons sherry
6 tablespoons water
4 tablespoons cornstarch
2 teaspoons sesame oil
4 tablespoons hoisin sauce
4 tablespoons salad oil
12 dried hot red chilis
4 garlic cloves, minced
1½ cups green onions, sliced
16 ounces water chestnuts, sliced

1) Mix the soy sauce, sherry, water, and cornstarch togethe. Add the chicken, mix well, cover, and let stand for 1 hour.

2) Remove the chicken, drain, and set aside. Stir the sesame oil and hoisin sauce into the marinade, and set aside.

3) Place a wok over a high flame. When wok is hot, add the oil. Place chicken in hot oil and cook, stirring quickly for 3 to 5 minutes, until browned. Remove and set aside.

4) Place the chilis in the wok, cook until black. Add the garlic and onions. Cook, stirring quickly for 30 seconds. Return the chicken to pan, add the water chestnuts and marinade, and cook, stirring quickly, until the sauce begins to thicken.

Serves 6

Roast Chicken and Pecans

3 pound roasting chicken
dash of salt
dash of pepper
¾ cup celery, chopped
¾ cup onion, chopped
½ tablespoon butter
⅓ cup pecans, chopped
2 cups cooked rice
1 tablespoon marjoram
1 tablespoon thyme

1) Lightly season the chicken with salt and pepper.

2) Saute the celery and onion in butter until tender. Add the pecans and continue to saute for 3 additional minutes. Toss with cooked rice, marjoram, and thyme. Stuff the chicken with the mixture.

3) Roast chicken at 350 degrees for 1½ hours, basting often with the pan juices.

Serves 4

Baked Chicken and Vegetables

4 2-pound broilers, cut in half lengthwise
12 potatoes, peeled and quartered
6 onions, peeled and quartered
6 baby carrots, peeled and sliced
1 teaspoon salt
1 teaspoon pepper
2 cups half and half cream
⅓ pound butter

1) Lay the vegetables on the bottom of a roasting pan and place the chicken on top of the vegetables.

2) Season the chicken with the salt and pepper, and then pour the cream over the top. Dot with butter, cover, and bake in a 350 degree oven for 1¼ hour.

3) Remove and place under a broiler, uncovered, for 5 to 10 minutes.

Serves 8

Chicken and Artichoke Surprise

2 3-pound chickens, quartered
4 tablespoons butter, melted
¾ cup white wine
dash of salt
dash of pepper
24 ounces artichoke hearts
3 tablespoons parsley, chopped

1) Brown the chicken in the melted butter. Add the wine, salt, and pepper. Cover and let cook for 30 minutes.

2) Add the artichoke hearts, cover, and cook for an additional 20 minutes. Top with parsley and serve.

Serves 6

Chicken Fried in Buttermilk

3 pound fryer, cut into serving sized pieces
1 cup flour
1 teaspoon salt
1½ teaspoons paprika
½ teaspoon pepper
¾ cup buttermilk
fat

1) Mix the flour, paprika, salt, and pepper together. Dip the chicken in buttermilk and roll in the dry mixture. Fry the coated chicken in hot fat for 10 to 12 minutes.

2) Place the fried chicken, covered, in a 350 degree oven for 30 minutes.

Serves 4

Chicken and Rice

2 chicken breasts, cut in half
¼ teaspoon salt
¼ teaspoon pepper
¼ teaspoon all-purpose seasoning
½ cup flour
¼ cup peanut oil
¾ cup instant rice
6 ounces cream of chicken soup
½ cup half and half cream

1) Lightly season the chicken with the salt, pepper and seasoning. Coat the seasoned chicken in the flour. Brown the coated chicken in hot oil.

2) Cook the rice. Add the cream and the chicken soup to the rice. Place the rice mixture into an oiled casserole dish and set the pieces of chicken on top. Bake at 350 degrees 30 minutes.

Serves 4

Glazed Chicken

2 3-pound broilers, quartered
¾ cup honey
4 tablespoons lime juice
dash of garlic salt
3 tablespoons Dijon mustard

1) Mix the honey and lime juice together. Lightly season the chicken with garlic salt. Spread 1½ tablespoons Dijon on chicken and broil for 20 minutes, basting with ½ of the honey mixture.

2) Turn the chicken over, spread with remaining Dijon and broil for an additional 20 minutes, basting with the remaining honey mixture.

Serves 6

TURKEY

Smoked Drumsticks
with Peppercorns

3 pounds turkey drumsticks, smoked
water
8 peppercorns
2 bay leaves
2 slices onion
⅔ cup sour cream
3 tablespoons horseradish
dash of pepper

1) Place the turkey drumsticks in enough boiling water to cover. Add the peppercorns, bay leaves, and slices of onion. Bring to boil, lower the flame, and simmer for 45 minutes. Remove from the water.

2) Mix the horseradish, sour cream, and pepper together. Slice off the meat from the drumsticks, removing the bones and tendons and serve.

Serves 6

Turkey Wings in Teriyaki Sauce

8 pounds turkey wings
oil
½ cup sherry
4 cups soy sauce
4 garlic cloves, minced
2 tablespoons orange rind, grated
4 tablespoons ginger root, minced

1) Divide each wing into three sections, coat with oil, and place in a single layer in a roasting pan. Roast uncovered in a preheated 375 degree oven for 45 minutes.

2) Mix the remaining ingredients together and spoon over the turkey. Cover with foil and cook for an additional 45 minutes.

Serves 8

Mexican Turkey

2 cups cooked turkey, diced
6 ounces spicy enchilada sauce
2 cups chicken broth
3 ounces evaporated milk
8 corn tortillas
¾ cup Jack cheese, shredded
⅓ cup onions, chopped
3 ounces green chilis, drained, seeded and chopped

1) Preheat oven at 350 degrees.

2) Mix the enchilada sauce, chicken broth, and milk together.

3) Lay 4 tortillas on the bottom of a well oiled baking pan. Place the turkey on top of the tortillas. Top with ⅔ cup cheese, onions, and chilis.

4) Place the remaining tortillas on top and sprinkle with the remaining cheese. Pour the enchilada sauce over everything and bake for 1 hour, basting once or twice during cooking.

Serves 4

Roast Turkey in Apricot Brandy

6 pound turkey
½ teaspoon salt
½ teaspoon pepper
2 tablespoons apricot brandy
2 tablespoons white wine
2 tablespoons butter, melted
½ teaspoon dried basil
½ teaspoon dried thyme

1) Remove the neck and giblets from the turkey. Rinse turkey in cold water and pat dry with paper towels.

2) Rub the salt and pepper into the cavity of the turke, close with skewers and tie the drumstick ends to the tail. Brush the turkey with the melted butter and place in a roasting pan.

3) Mix the remaining ingredients together and spoon over turkey. Place in a 325 degree oven for 2 hours, basting often. Cut the string holding the drumsticks to the tail and cook for an additional 1 hour until drumsticks move easily.

Serves 10

Herbed Turkey Thighs

2½ pounds turkey thighs
2 garlic cloves, minced
2 tablespoons oregano
4 peppercorns
⅓ cup olive oil
¾ cup lemon juice
1½ cups chicken broth
2 tablespoons flour

1) Mix the garlic, oregano, peppercorns, oil and lemon juice together. Place the turkey in a baking dish and pour the mixture over the top. Cover the refrigerate overnight, turning occasionally.

2) Remove from marinade and place in a preheated 325 degree oven for 30 minutes. Remove, turn over, baste, and bake for an additional 25 minutes.

3) Drain the fat from the baking dish and place in a pot medium flame. Add the flour and cook for one minute, stirring often. Slowly add the chicken broth and continue to cook, stirring the whole time, until it is smooth and rich. Pour over turkey thighs.

Serves 4

Turkey Croquettes

5 cups turkey, chopped
2 onions, chopped
¼ teaspoon nutmeg
¼ teaspoon salt
¼ teaspoon pepper
3 tablespoons butter, melted
6 tablespoons flour
3 cups heavy cream
4 eggs, beaten
bread crumbs
fat

1) Mix the turkey, onion, and seasonings together. Blend the melted butter and flour together, add to the cream, and cook over a low flame until smooth.

2) Combine the turkey mixture to the cream mixture. Chill.

3) Form the chilled mixture into croquettes, coat with the egg, roll in the bread crumbs, and fry in fat until crispy.

Serves 8

Chilled Turkey Mold

1 cup cooked turkey, diced
½ envelope gelatin
2 tablespoons cold water
1 bouillon cube
¼ cup boiling water
½ tablespoon lemon juice
¼ teaspoon Tabasco sauce
¼ cup mayonnaise
¼ teaspoon paprika
½ teaspoon onion, grated
½ teaspoon salt
¾ cup cottage cheese
2 tablespoons celery, diced
2 tablespoons green pepper, chopped
2 tablespoons pimiento, chopped

1) Place gelatin in cold water until soft. Dissolve bouillon cube in boiling water, pour into softened gelatin and stir until dissolved. Let cool.

2) Add the lemon juice, Tabasco sauce, mayonnaise, paprika, onion, and salt. Beat the cottage cheese until rich and creamy. Add to the gelatin mixture. Fold in the turkey, celery, green pepper, and pimiento. Pour into a mold and chill until firm.

Serves 4

Lemon Turkey with Parsley

1½ pound turkey cutlets, ¼ inch thick
2 tablespoons butter, melted
½ cup lemon juice
pinch of salt
pinch of pepper
4 tablespoons parsley, chopped

1) Saute the cutlets in melted butter over a low flame for 6 minutes, turning once. Remove and keep warm. Stir in the lemon juice, salt, and pepper to the butter and bring to a boil. Spoon over the turkey. Sprinkle with parsley and serve.

Serves 6

Turkey Marsala

2 pound boned turkey breast, skinned, cut, and
pounded into ⅛ inch thick slices
flour
¾ cup butter
1 pound mushrooms
1 cup Marsala
¼ teaspoon salt
¼ teaspoon pepper
½ pound prosciutto, sliced thinly
2 cups Swiss cheese, shredded
cooked peas

1) Coat turkey pieces in flour. Lightly brown the turkey in
¼ cup of butter. Remove and keep warm.

2) Lightly brown the mushroom in the same pan. Pour
in the Marsala, stir, and then remove mushrooms and
place next to the turkey.

3) Heat the pan juices until boiling and add remaining
butter, salt, and pepper, stirring until well blended.
Remove and keep warm.

4) Place prosciutto and Swiss cheese on top of turkey.
Broil until the cheese melts. Spoon sauce around the
edge of the dish, place peas around the turkey and
serve.

Serves 6

Rosemary Wings

8 pounds turkey wings, separated at joints
8 tablespoons butter, melted
1 tablespoon fresh rosemary, crushed
1 teaspoon salt
½ teaspoon pepper

1) Mix the rosemary, salt, and pepper into the hot, melted butter.

2) Place the turkey wings in a single layer in an oiled, shallow baking pan. Coat the wings with the herb mixture. Place in a preheated 350 degree oven for 30 minutes. Turn over, baste, and cook for an additional 25 minutes.

Makes 8 servings

Tasty Turkey Hash

2 cups cooked turkey, diced
3 tablespoons butter, melted
½ green pepper, seeded, chopped
⅓ cup onion, chopped
1 large garlic cloves, chopped
¾ cup cooked stuffing
pinch of salt
pinch of pepper
⅓ cup almonds, toasted
½ cup black olives, pitted
½ cup heavy cream

1) Lightly brown the green pepper, onion, and garlic. Mix in the turkey, stuffing, salt, and pepper. Cook until completely warm.

2) Flip over, mix in the almonds and olives, spoon cream over the top, cook until the bottom of the hash becomes crispy.

Serves 4

Dijon Turkey

8 turkey cutlets, ¼ inch thick
flour
1½ tablespoon oil
1½ tablespoon butter
4 tablespoons shallots, minced
½ cup white wine
⅔ cup cream
½ teaspoon salt
½ teaspoon pepper
2 tablespoons Dijon mustard

1) Lightly dust the turkey with flour. Lightly brown in oil and butter. Remove and keep warm.

2) Place more oil and butter in the pan, add the shallots, and cook quickly for one minute. Add the wine and cook until the wine is almost completely evaporated. Stir constantly.

3) Add the cream, salt, and pepper and cook until the mixture begins to bubble. Remove from heat and add the Dijon. Spoon over the warm turkey cutlets and serve.

Serves 8

Light and Fluffy Turkey Souffle

3 tablespoons butter, melted
¼ cup flour
1 cup milk
¼ teaspoon salt
¾ cup cooked turkey, chopped
2 eggs, separated

1) Place flour and melted butter over a low flame and stir until smooth. Slowly add the milk, raise flame to medium level and cook until thick. Remove from heat and mix in the turkey and salt.

2) Beat the egg yolks and slowly mix in ⅓ of the turkey mixture. Mix the egg and turkey mixture into the remaining hot mixture.

3) Beat the egg whites and gently fold into the turkey mixture. Pour into a lightly oiled souffle dish and place in a 325 degree oven for 45 minutes.

Serves 4

Indian Turkey

4 cups diced cooked turkey
5 tablespoons butter, melted
1 cup onions, chopped
2 apples, seeded and chopped
4 celery ribs, sliced thinly
5 tablespoons flour
4 tablespoons curry powder
½ teaspoon ginger
2 teaspoons cumin
2½ cups chicken broth

1) Saute the apples, onions, and celery until soft. Stir in the flour and then add curry, ginger, and cumin.

2) Slowly stir in the chicken broth until the mixture is smooth and rich. Mix in the turkey, lower the flame, and simmer for an additional 5 minutes.

Serves 8

Turkey Curry with Almonds

6 cups cooked turkey, diced
½ cup oil
2 celery stalks, sliced diagonally
2 green peppers, sliced
2 bunches green onions, sliced diagonally
4 tablespoons almonds, salted and slivered
4 cups water chestnuts, sliced
6 tablespoons flour
2 teaspoons flour
2 teaspoons curry powder
1 teaspoon basil
2 teaspoons paprika
3 cups chicken broth
2 cups pineapple tidbits, drained
½ cup pimiento, chopped

1) Brown the celery, peppers, and onions in hot oil. Add turkey, almonds, and water chestnuts. Stir in the flour, curry, basil, and paprika. Cook until well blended.

2) Mix in the chicken broth, pineapple, and pimientos. cover and cook for 3 minutes.

Serves 8

Broiled Turkey
with Pineapple Chunks

2 pounds boned turkey breast, skinned and cut into chunks
½ cup butter, melted
½ teaspoon dry rosemary
½ teaspoon dry thyme
½ teaspoon sage
½ teaspoon paprika
¼ cup sherry
2½ pound pineapple, peeled, cored and cut into chunks

1) Mix the butter, rosemary, thyme, sage, paprika and sherry together. Coat turkey with mixture. Cover and let marinate for 1 hour.

2) Remove the turkey from the marinade and drain, reserving marinade. Thread turkey and pineapple chunks on skewers, place on a broiler rack and cook for 8 minutes, basting often. Turn and cook for an additional 8 minutes, continuing to baste.

Serves 4

Italian Turkey Wings

6 pounds turkey wings, separated at joints
2 teaspoons paprika
2 teaspoons savory
2 cups flour
1 teaspoon salt
1 teaspoon pepper
¾ cup butter, melted
2 cups buttermilk
⅔ cup Parmesan cheese, grated

1) Mix the dry ingredients together. Coat the wings in buttermilk, then roll them in the dry mixture. Brush with the melted and place in a baking dish in a single layer.

2) Bake in a 325 degree oven for 1¾ hours.

Serves 8

Turkey with Wild Rice and Mushrooms

2 cups cooked turkey, diced
¾ cup wild rice, washed, soaked, and drained
¾ pound mushrooms, sliced
1 onion, chopped
4 tablespoons butter
⅓ cup almonds, blanched and sliced
1 teaspoon salt
¼ teaspoon pepper
1 cup heavy cream
2 cups chicken broth
2 tablespoons Parmesan cheese, grated

1) Lightly brown the mushrooms and onions in 2 tablespoons. Place in an oiled casserole dish. Add the turkey, rice, almonds, salt and pepper. Stir in the cream and chicken broth.

2) Cover and bake in a preheated 350 degree oven for 1¼ hours. Remove cover, sprinkle with Parmesan cheese, and dot with the remaining butter. Increase the oven temperature to 450 degrees and bake for an additional 5 to 10 minutes.

Serves 4

Turkey with Raisins and Almonds

3 cups cooked turkey, diced
2 tablespoons butter, melted
1½ cups bulgur wheat
½ cup onions, minced
3 cups chicken broth
3 tablespoons golden raisins
⅓ cup almonds, sliced
1 teaspoon oregano
dash of salt
dash of pepper

1) Saute the onions and wheat in the melted butter until onions are transparent. Add the chicken broth, raisins, almonds, oregano, salt, and pepper and bring to boil.

2) Lower the flame, cover, and simmer for 10 minutes. Mix in the turkey, cover, and cook for an additional 5 minutes.

Serves 8

Turkey with White Sauce

3 cups cooked turkey, chopped
3 tablespoons butter, melted
1 cup celery, chopped
4 tablespoons flour
3 cups milk
1 teaspoon salt
½ teaspoon pepper
½ cup breadcrumbs

1) Saute the celery in melted butter for 5 minutes. Blend in the flour, stirring until smooth. Slowly add the milk, and cook over a medium flame, stirring until the mixture is thick. Stir in the turkey, salt, and pepper to the sauce.

2) Spoon the sauce into a lightly oiled casserole dish and top with breadcrumbs. Place in an oven at 400 degrees for 30 minutes.

Serves 8

Turkey Karma

4 cups cooked turkey, diced
1½ tablespoon butter
3 tablespoons oil
2 cups onions, chopped
2 garlic cloves, crushed
2 tablespoons flour
1½ cups chicken broth
1 teaspoon ginger
½ teaspoon cinnamon
1 teaspoon cardamom, ground
few drops of Tabasco sauce
2 cups plain yogurt

1) Saute the onions in butter and oil until transparent. Stir in the garlic. Stir in the flour. Add the chicken broth and cook until the mixture begins to thicken. Stir often.

2) Lower the flame and add the ginger, cinnamon, cardamom, Tabasco sauce, and turkey. Cover and simmer over a low flame for 5 minutes. Add the yogurt, mixing well, and serve.

Serves 8

Lemon Turkey with Capers

2 pounds boned turkey breast, skinned, cut, and pounded into ⅛ inch thick slices
flour
¾ cup butter
¼ teaspoon salt
¼ teaspoon pepper
4 tablespoons lemon juice
1 cup water
2 teaspoons capers

1) Coat turkey pieces in flour. Lightly brown the turkey in ¼ cup of butter. Remove and keep warm.

2) Place lemon juice, water, and capers in pan, and heat until boiling and add remaining butter, salt, and pepper, stirring until well blended. Remove and keep warm. Spoon sauce over the turkey and serve.

Serves 6

Wings with Mushrooms and Sweet Peppers

6 pounds turkey wings, separated at joints
2 tablespoons butter
2 tablespoons oil
2 onions, sliced
1 pound mushrooms, sliced
2 cups chicken broth
2 cups sweet red peppers, sliced
4 tablespoons parsley, chopped
½ teaspoon salt
½ teaspoon pepper

1) Brown the wings in butter and oil. Remove from pan. Saute the mushrooms in the same pan until transparent. Remove mushrooms, add butter and oil, and lightly saute the onions.

2) Remove onions, return the browned wings to the pan, and place the mushrooms and onions on top. Add the chicken broth, sweet pepper, parsley, salt and pepper.

3) Simmer over a low flame, covered, for 1 hour. Turn and cook for an additional 45 minutes.

Serves 8

Fried Turkey

8 pounds turkey drumsticks, thighs, and wings
⅔ cup flour
1 teaspoon paprika
½ teaspoon pepper
4 tablespoons milk
4 eggs
⅔ cup Parmesan cheese, grated
4 cups croutons, crushed
½ cup butter, melted

1) Mix the flour, paprika, and pepper together. Beat milk and eggs together. Mix the cheese and croutons together.

2) Coat the turkey pieces in the flour mixture, dip in egg mixture, drain, and roll in crouton mixture. Place on a baking pan and cover with foil.

3) Place in a 350 degree oven for 1½ hours. Remove foil, dot the turkey with butter. Bake uncovered for an additional 20 minutes.

Serves 8

Turkey with Maple Syrup

1 pound boneless white meat turkey roast, frozen
¼ cup maple syrup

1) Coat the roast with syrup, reserving 2 tablespoons. Place in a baking dish, cover with foil, and bake in a 400 degree oven for 30 minutes.

2) Baste, cover, and cook for an additional 30 minutes. Add remaining maple syrup and cook for an additional 30 minutes. Let stand for 20 minutes and serve.

Serves 4

DUCK

Broiled Black Duck

6 black ducks, split and opened
3 lemons
⅓ pound of butter, melted
4 jiggers of applejack
dash of salt
dash of pepper

1) Mix the melted butter, the applejack, and the juice of two lemons together. Lightly season the duck with salt and pepper then coat with the butter mixture.

2) Place on a preheated broiler, baste and turn often for approximately 15 minutes.

Serves 6

Traditional Roast Duck

6 pound duck
salt
pepper

1) Rub the cavity of the duck with salt and pepper. With a fork, punch holes in the skin. Place in a preheated 450 degree oven on a rack in a roasting pan.

2) Cook for 45 minutes then turn the breast over. Cook for an additional 45 minutes and turn over again. Baste with ¼ cup cold water and allow to cook for an additional 30 minutes. Baste often while cooking.

Serves 6

Short Cut Orange Duck

6 pound duck
2 garlic cloves
3 oranges, peeled and separated
dash of salt
dash of pepper
1½ cups orange juice
⅓ cup orange liqueur
1½ tablespoon orange zest, grated
1½ teaspoons butter

1) Place the orange sections and the garlic inside of the duck. Rub the skin with salt and pepper. Place the duck on a rack in a roasting pan and cook for 2 hours in a preheated 350 degree oven. Baste often with the orange juice. Remove duck and keep warm.

2) Skim the fat from the roasting pan, add the orange liqueur, orange zest, and remaining orange juice. Cook over a high flame until it begins to thicken. Add butter, salt, pepper. Serve the duck with the oranges and the sauce.

Serves 6

Stuffed Black Duck

3 black ducks
¾ cabbage head, shredded
3 carrots, grated
4 onions, shredded
¾ teaspoon ground dill
¾ teaspoon powdered savory
⅛ pound of butter, melted
2 eggs, separated
1½ tablespoons Worcestershire sauce
1½ wineglass sherry
1½ cups breadcrumbs
dash of salt
dash of pepper
6 strips of bacon
6 ounces white wine

1) Mix the cabbage, carrots, onions, dill, and savory together. Add ⅛ pound of melted butter, the egg yolks, Worcestershire, sherry, breadcrumbs, salt, and pepper. Stuff the ducks with the mixture.

2) Rub stuffed ducks with salt and pepper and cover each breast with two strips of bacon. Place in a preheated 350 degree oven and cook for 30 minutes. Baste often with a mixture of remaining butter and white wine.

Serves 6

Duck with Ham and Black Olives

6 pound duck, roasted and carved into serving
sized pieces
4 tablespoons butter, melted
4 tablespoons ham, chopped
2 carrots, chopped
1½ tablespoon onion, chopped
2 celery ribs, chopped
5 tablespoons flour
2½ cups beef broth
¼ teaspoon mace
dash of powdered cloves
1 bay leaf
3 parsley sprigs
18 black olives, pitted
4 tablespoons dry sherry
pinch of salt

1) Place the ham, carrots, onions, and celery in the
melted butter. Cook until the vegetables begin to
brown, stirring often. Mix in the flour. When browned,
gradually add the broth, mace, cloves, bay leaf, and
parsley. Cook for an additional 5 minutes, stirring often.

2) Strain the sauce and return to saucepan. Add the
duck, olives, sherry, and salt. Cook until completely
warm. Place the duck on a platter, surround with olives,
and coat with glaze.

Serves 6

Duck with Sauerkraut and Wine

6 pound duck
½ cup salt pork, diced
1½ apples, chopped
1½ onions, chopped
sprig of thyme
caraway seeds
pinch of salt
pinch of pepper
2 pounds sauerkraut
white wine

1) Place pork, apple, and onion in a pan and saute for 3 minutes. Add thyme, caraway seeds, salt, and pepper. Mix in the sauerkraut. Stuff the ducks with the mixture, sewing up the openings.

2) Place the ducks on a rack in a roasting pan and place in a preheated 350 degree oven for 2 hours. Baste often with wine. Remove and keep warm.

3) Skim the fat from the pan juices, cook for a few minutes and pour over duck.

Serves 6

Spicy Duck

6 black ducks
⅛ pound of butter
6 tablespoons Worcestershire sauce
6 squirts Tabasco sauce
3 tablespoons black currant jelly
6 ounces dry sherry
2 carrots
6 shallots
1½ tablespoons chopped parsley
½ teaspoon marjoram
dash of salt
dash of pepper

1) Rub the ducks with salt and pepper and place them in a preheated 425 degree oven for 15 minutes. Remove from oven, remove the skin, and cut ¼" slices from the breast. Set aside.

2) Place the ducks into a press and extract the juices. Melt 2 ounces of butter and add the Worcestershire sauce, Tabasco sauce, black currant jelly, and the duck extract. Mix well, add the duck breast, cover, and simmer over a low flame for 5 minutes.

3) Place 2 ounces of butter in another pan and add the liver. When brown, add the sherry, carrots, shallots, parsley, marjoram, salt, and pepper, and simmer over a low flame for an additional ten minutes.

4) Strain the liver mixture and add to the duck breast sauce. Mix well. Simmer over a low flame for an additional five minutes, uncovered.

Serves 6

Orange Duck

6 pound duck
pinch of salt
pinch of pepper
6 oranges
2 lemons
3 tablespoons sugar
4 tablespoons wine vinegar
2½ cups beef broth
1½ tablespoons cornstarch
2½ tablespoons red currant jelly
4 tablespoons white wine

1) Rub the inside of the duck with salt and pepper. Punch holes into the skin with a fork. Roast for 2 hours in a preheated 350 degree oven on a rack in a roasting pan.

2) Peel the colored edge of 2 oranges and 1 lemon and cut into thin strips. Squeeze the juice from the peeled fruit and set aside. Place the strips in boiling water, steep for 5 minutes, drain and let stand. Separate sections of the remaining oranges and lemon, place in a bowl and let stand.

3) Melt the sugar over a medium flame until it turns a golden color. Add the orange juice, lemon juice, and vinegar, bring to a boil, and cook until mixture

is reduced by half. Mix in the broth and simmer for an additional 5 minutes.

4) Dissolve the cornstarch in 3 teaspoons of water. Add to the sugar mixture and combine with the currant jelly, mixing until the sauce is clear and thick.

5) When the duck is done, remove and keep warm. Skim fat from the pan and place over a high flame. Add the wine, mix, and boil quickly for 1 minute. Strain into sauce. Sprinkle the duck with strips of rind, arrange fruit around duck and glaze the duck with the sauce.

Serves 6

Duck with Peppercorns

6 pound duck, split in half and wings removed
1 lemon
1 teaspoon salt
2 tablespoons black peppercorns, crushed

1) Rub the duck with lemon and lightly season with salt. Place on a rack in a broiling pan and cook for 25 minutes.

2) Turn over, punch the skin with a fork, and broil for an additional 15 minutes. Remove and press crused peppercorns into the skin. Broil, skin side up, for an additional 15 minutes until crispy.

Serves 4

Browned Duck with Green Olives

6 pound duck, pricked with a fork
2 tablespoons butter, melted
2 cups chicken broth
¾ cup Port wine
2 celery ribs with leaves, chopped
6 parsley sprigs
1 bay leaf
3 teaspoons thyme, crumbled
18 green olives
dash of salt
dash of pepper

1) Brown the duck in melted butter. Drain the fat, and mix in the chicken broth, wine, celery, parsley, bay leaf, and thyme. Cover and simmer over a low flame for 1¼ hours.

2) Simmer the olives in another pan for 5 minutes, drain, let stand. Remove the duck and keep warm. Strain the pan liquid, place back in the pan, and boil quickly over a high flame until reduced by one third. Lightly season with salt and pepper.

3) Carve the duck, arrange olives around the platter and spoon the broth all over.

Serves 6

GOOSE

Leftover Goose

**2 cups leftover meat, bones and gravy from
a roasted goose
1½ cups water
2 onions, chopped
4 tablespoons butter
1 cup leftover stuffing
dash of salt
dash of pepper**

1) Dice the goose meat and let stand. Place gravy
and bones in a pot, add water, and simmer over a
low flame for 15 minutes.

2) Saute the onions in the butter, then add the
goose meat, leftover stuffing, salt, and pepper.
Pour ½ cup goose broth into pan and simmer over
low flame, stirring often. Cook until almost dry.

Serves 4

Cassoulet

6 pound goose
½ quart navy beans
⅛ pound Italian salami, cubed
2 onions, diced
2 peppercorns
1 garlic clove, minced
¼ teaspoon rosemary
1 bay leaf
1 teaspoon chopped parsley
1½ cups white wine
dash of salt
dash of pepper
2 ounces olive oil

1) Soak the navy beans overnight. Drain and add the salami, onions, peppercorns, garlic, rosemary, bay leaf, and parsley. Cover with water. Cover tightly and place in a 250 degree oven for 4 hours.

2) Two hours before mixture is ready, cut the goose into 6 sections. Rub the goose with salt and pepper. Saute the goose in hot oil until it begins to brown. Lower the flame and add the wine, cover, and simmer over medium flame for 25 minutes. Remove the casserole and add to the duck, mixing well. Cover and place in the oven for an additional 1 to 1½ hours.

Serves 4

Goose, Prunes, and Apples

6 pound goose
18 prunes, pitted
¾ cup red wine
dash of salt
dash of pepper
4 green apples, peeled, cored and quartered
1½ tablespoons flour
1 cup chicken broth

1) Soak the prunes in the red wine for 30 minutes. Rub the goose with salt and pepper. Drain the prunes, mix with the pieces of apple and stuff into the goose opening.

2) Sew up the cavity. Punch the goose with a fork. Place the goose on a rack in a pan and cook in a 325 degree oven for 2¾ hours.

3) Skim the fat, reserving 1 tablespoon. Mix reserved fat with flour and cook until it begins to brown. Gradually add the chicken broth, cooking until thick. Stir often. Lightly season with salt and pepper. Serve with goose.

Serves 4

Grab Bag Goose

6 pound goose
1 onion, sliced
1 tablespoon butter
½ cup water
1 cup white wine
½ pound slab bacon in 1 piece
1½ pounds sauerkraut
6 juniper berries, tied in a cheesecloth bag
1 garlic clove, minced
pinch of salt
pinch of pepper
⅛ cup celery, diced
⅛ cup carrots, diced
⅛ cup leek, diced
4 frankfurters, heated

1) Saute the onion in the goose fat. Add the water and wine. Place the bacon, sauerkraut, berries, garlic, salt, and pepper in the liquid, cover and cook over a low flame for 1½ hours. Remove the cheesecloth bag.

2) Cook the goose in a preheated 400 degree oven for 2 hours. Add the vegetables to the roasting pan and cook for an additional 30 minutes.

3) Place the sauerkraut on a large serving platter. Arrange the goose, bacon, and frankfurters on top of the sauerkraut. Strain fat from pan juices, add 3 tablespoons broth and heat. Spoon vegetables and juices over the meats.

Serves 4

Goose and Pork Sausage

6 pound goose
1 pound pork sausage
3 cups breadcrumbs
½ cup celery, chopped
⅓ cup onion, chopped

1) Punch the goose with a fork. Mix the remaining ingredients together and stuff into the inside of the goose. Close the opening with skewers.

2) Bake, uncovered, in a 450 degree oven for 10 minutes. Lower heat to 350 degrees and bake for 1½ hours. Baste often.

Serves 4

Lemon Herb Goose

4 pound goose, cut into serving sized pieces
1 small onion, stuck with 2 cloves
½ sprig parsley
½ teaspoon dried thyme
1 lemon slice
dash of salt
dash of pepper
cold water to cover
1 egg yolk, beaten
½ cup cream

1) Place the goose, onion, parsley, thyme, lemon, salt, and pepper in a pot. Cover with boiling water and simmer over a low flame for 1½ hours. Remove the goose and keep warm.

2) Skim the fat from the broth and strain. Place 1 cup of broth over a high flame and bring to a boil. Lower flame, simmer for 5 minutes and add the egg yolk and cream. Stir until smooth and rich. Spoon over the goose.

Serves 4

Apple Goose

10 pound goose
½ teaspoon salt
½ teaspoon pepper
2 onions, chopped
¾ cup butter
5 cups breadcrumbs
5 cups apples, chopped
6 eggs, beaten
½ teaspoon salt
¼ teaspoon pepper

1) Punch goose with a fork. Rub the salt and pepper all over the goose. Let stand.

2) Saute the onion in butter until transparent. Stir in the remaining ingredients. Pour the sauce into the opening of the goose. Close the opening. Form small balls with remaining dressing, cover and refrigerate.

3) Place the goose on a rack in a roasting pan and cook uncovered in a 325 degree oven for 3 hours, until the drumsticks easily move. Place the stuffing balls in the roasting pan and cook for an additional 30 minutes.

Serves 8

Goose with Spinach

4 cups roasted goose, chopped
6 tablespoons butter
2 green peppers, seeded and chopped
2 onions, chopped
3 pounds potatoes, boiled, peeled and diced
dash of salt
dash of pepper
20 ounces frozen chopped spinach, cooked and drained
8 eggs
½ cup milk

1) Saute the pepper and onion in fat until onions are transparent. Mix in the goose and potatoes. Add salt and pepper, cover and cook over a medium flame for 20 minutes, stirring often until browned.

2) Stir in the spinach. Mix the eggs and the milk together and pour over the goose. Cover and simmer over low flame until the goose is firm.

Serves 8

Roast Goose with Peanuts

6 pound goose
¾ cup dry roasted peanuts, chopped
1½ cups cooked mashed potatoes
¾ cup breadcrumbs
1 teaspoon sage
1½ tablespoon onion juice
1 teaspoon salt
½ teaspoon pepper
⅔ cup butter, melted

1) Mix the peanuts, potatoes, breadcrumbs, sage, onion juice, salt, pepper, and ⅓ cup butter together. Set aside.

2) Punch the goose with a fork. Stuff the dressing into the opening of the goose, then close with skewers. Lightly season with remaining salt. Place the goose in a roasting pan and bake at 375 degrees for 2 hours until drumsticks move easily. Baste often with melted butter while cooking.

Serves 4

Goose with Vegetables

8 pound goose with giblets and neck
¼ cup butter, melted
3 carrots, peeled and sliced
3 celery ribs, chopped
1 onion, peeled sliced
3 garlic cloves, minced
2 bay leaves
1½ teaspoons dried thyme
¾ pound mushrooms, sliced
pinch of salt
pinch of pepper
⅓ cup flour
1½ cups port wine
3 cups chicken stock
¾ cup chopped fresh parsley

1) Saute the carrots, celery, onion, and garlic for 5 minutes. Add the bay leaves and thyme and saute for an additional 10 minutes. Chop the goose giblets and add to the vegetables. Add the mushrooms and cook an additional 10 minutes. Mix in the parsley and remove from heat.

2) Rub the goose with salt and pepper. Pour ⅓ of the vegetable mixture into the cavity. Close the

opening, and place the goose in a roasting pan. Cook in a preheated 450 degree oven for 20 minutes.

3) Stir in the flour to the remaining vegetable mixture and cook until thick. Pour in the port and chicken stock and heat to boiling.

4) Reduce the temperature of the oven to 350 degrees. Remove the goose, pour the vegetable mixture around the goose and continue cooking for an additional 2 hours, basting often.

5) Remove the goose, discard the vegetables from the cavity, carve and serve meat with vegetables.

Serves 6

SQUAB

Sauteed Squab

8 tablespoons butter, melted
8 squabs, split down the back and
pounded flat
dash of salt
dash of pepper
½ cup shallots, chopped
3 cups white wine
½ cup chopped parsley
4 tablespoons fresh tarragon

1) Brown the squabs in butter over a medium flame. Lightly season with salt and pepper.

2) Place half of the shallots and 1 cup of wine in the pan. Lower the heat, cover, and simmer for 15 minutes. Place parsley and tarragon in the pan. Add remaining wine and cook, uncovered, for 5 minutes. Spoon sauce over squab and serve.

Serves 8

Fried Squab

4 squabs, split
1 teaspoon salt
1 teaspoon pepper
¾ cup flour
3 cups shortening

1) Lightly season the squabs with salt and pepper. Coat with flour.

2) Fry the seasoned squabs in hot shortening for 15 to 20 minutes, turning frequently. Drain and serve.

Serves 4

Squab and Wild Rice

4 squabs
3 ounces foie gras
2 truffles
2 tablespoons butter
1¼ cups cooked wild rice
dash of salt
dash of pepper
¼ cup butter, melted
½ cup boiling water

1) Dice the foie gras and truffles and saute in 2 tablespoons melted butter. Mix the rice, salt, and pepper.

2) Stuff the squabs with mixture and close. Brush with melted butter and bake in a 400 degree oven for 45 minutes basting often with a mixture of melted butter and boiling water.

Serves 4

Squab and Plum Tomato Casserole

6 squabs
2 20-ounce cans plum tomatoes, pureed
7 small onions
6 tablespoons butter
dash of salt
dash of pepper
12 parsley sprigs
8 bacon slices, diced
1½ garlic cloves, chopped
2 onions, chopped
1½ cups mushrooms, sliced
¼ teaspoon dried thyme
¼ teaspoon dried sweet basil

1) Cook tomato puree over a medium flame with 1 chopped onion until thick. Add the butter, salt, and pepper.

2) Stuff the squabs with the small onions and sprigs of parsley. Brown the bacon. Remove the bacon and brown the squab and garlic.

3) Place the squabs in a casserole dish with the mushrooms, onion, thyme, basil, and tomato sauce. Cover and simmer in a preheated 350 degree oven for 1 hour.

Serves 6

Squab with Mushrooms

4 squabs
1 tablespoon butter or margarine, melted
2 slices bacon, diced
¾ cup onion, chopped
1 carrot, chopped
¼ teaspoon salt
½ cup mushrooms, sliced
¼ cup port wine

1) Saute the squabs, bacon, carrot, onion, and salt in butter until the squabs are lightly browned.

2) Add the wine and mushrooms, cover, and simmer over a low flame for 45 minutes. Pour sauce over squabs and serve.

Serves 4

PIGEON

Saffron Pigeon

8 pigeons
3 cups white wine
¼ teaspoon saffron
1 teaspoon rosemary
2 cups salted olives, chopped
2 cups cooked white rice
pinch of pepper
1 cup olive oil
2 cups sour cream

1) Place wine, saffron, rosemary, and olives in a pan and bring to a boil. Lower the flame and simmer for 5 minutes. Strain off the olives and reserve the liquid. Mix the olives with the rice, add pepper and stuff the pigeons with the mixture. Close cavity.

2) Rub the pigeons with olive oil and place them in a roasting pan. Add the remaining olive oil to the liquid mixture. Place the pigeons in a preheated 450 degree oven. Lower to 300 degrees and cook for 30 minutes, basting often with liquid mixture.

3) Remove pigeons and keep warm. Place roasting pan over a low flame, add the sour cream and stir until thick. Pour over pigeons and serve.

Serves 8

All-Purpose Pigeon

8 pigeons, split
1 teaspoon salt
1 teaspoon pepper
4 tablespoons butter, melted
4 tablespoons flour
4 cups beef broth
2 onions, sliced
1 cup mushrooms, sliced
4 whole cloves
2 bay leaves

1) Lightly season the pigeons with salt and pepper. Saute pigeons in melted butter until brown. Remove to a casserole dish, reserving drippings in the pan.

2) Add the flour to the pan drippings, stirring until rich and smooth. Place over a medium flame, add broth and cook until thick, stirring often. Mix in remaining salt and pepper. Add remaining ingredients and cook over medium flame until heated.

3) Pour the sauce over the pigeons and cook, covered, over a low flame for 45 minutes. Remove cloves and bay leaves and serve.

Serves 8

Pigeon Casserole

8 pigeons, split
1½ cups olive oil
dash of salt
dash of pepper
3 onions, chopped
3 cloves garlic, chopped
2 green peppers, seeded and sliced thinly
1 cup chicken broth
3 cups raw rice
1 cup mushrooms, sliced
5 pimientos, sliced thinly
1 cup pine nuts
chicken broth

1) Brown the pigeons in a casserole dish in 1 cup hot olive oil. Lightly season with salt and pepper and add green peppers, onions, garlic, and 1 cup chicken broth. Cover the dish and simmer in a preheated 350 degree oven for 1 hour.

2) Brown the rice in the remaining oil. Add browned rice and remaining ingredients to the casserole and cover with hot chicken broth. Place in oven, uncovered, and cook until the rice is soft and the broth has dissolved.

Serves 8

Herb Pigeon

6 pigeons, split
2 wineglasses applejack
flour
dash of salt
dash of pepper
¼ pound of butter, melted
2 cups mushrooms, sliced
¼ teaspoon ginger
½ teaspoon thyme
1½ tablespoons chopped parsley
1½ cups chicken stock
1½ cups rose wine
1½ tablespoons lemon juice
¾ cup orange juice

1) Coat pigeons with applejack. Dust with flour and lightly season with salt and pepper. Saute in melted butter until brown. Remove and keep warm.

2) Saute mushrooms in the butter until brown, return the pigeons to the pan and stir in ginger, thyme, parsley, salt, pepper, chicken stock, and rose wine. Bring to a boil, lower flame and simmer, covered, for 25 minutes. Mix in lemon and orange juice and simmer for an additional 5 minutes.

Serves 6

Pigeons Anna-Lisa

6 pigeon breasts
dash of salt
dash of pepper
6 bacon slices
¼ pound butter, melted
6 tablespoons flour
3 tablespoons melted butter
3 cups hot chicken consomme
¾ cup heavy cream
1 can white grapes, drained

1) Lightly season the breasts with salt and pepper and cover with a slice of bacon. Saute in melted butter until brown.

2) Mix flour and 3 tablespoons of melted butter together. Gradually heat, then slowly add the chicken consomme. Cook over low flame for 20 minutes, stirring often. Strain and add the cream and grapes. Reheat and pour over the pigeon breasts.

Serves 6

QUAIL

Simple Broiled Quail

8 quails, split
10 tablespoons butter, melted

1) Brush the quails with melted butter and place on a broiler rack and broil for 7 minutes on each side, basting often.

Serves 4

Baked Quails with Pears

4 large pears, halves, cored, and partially
hollowed out
ground cinnamon
8 quails
dash of salt
dash of pepper
½ cup dried currants
¾ cup brandy
¼ cup sweet mustard
1 cup heavy cream

1) Sprinkle the inside of the pear halves with cinnamon.
Lightly season the quail with salt and pepper and place
them in the pear halves. Sprinkle with currants and
pour brandy over all. Set aside for 1 hour.

2) Remove quails and pears. Drain the brandy and
reserve. Stuff the quails with the currants and spread
mustard over each quail. Place the pears in a roasting
pan and arrange each quail in a pear. Bake in a
preheated 425 degree oven for 30 minutes.

3) Remove and keep warm. Place ⅓ cup of brandy in
the pan drippings and heat over a medium flame. Stir
often, add cream and cook until thick. Mix in 1
tablespoon mustard and pour sauce over the quails.

Serves 4

Quail Hash

4 quails
2 onions, quartered
4 carrots, sliced
6 celery stalks, sliced
2 bay leaves
½ tablespoon thyme
1 teaspoon salt
1 teaspoon pepper
3 tablespoons sherry

1) Place the ingredients with the exception of the sherry in water to cover. Boil over a medium flame for 45 minutes. Bone the quail and slice the meat.

2) Mix the quail stock and sherry together. Add quail and serve.

Serves 4

Quail with Liver and Mushrooms

4 quail, split and flattened
⅛ pound butter, melted
2 chicken livers, chopped
4 mushroom caps
1 shallot, split
¼ teaspoon chervil
dash of salt
dash of pepper
⅓ cup of red wine
4 pieces toasted bread

1) Saute the shallot in one half of the melted butter until brown. Remove shallot, add mushrooms and saute until brown. Remove and set aside. Saute the chicken livers until brown. Add remaining ingredients, except the quail, and simmer over a low flame until liquid has dissolved. Mash liver.

2) Rub the quails with butter, salt and pepper and place in a roasting pan in a preheated broiler. Cook for 10 minutes, basting often. Place a mushroom cap on each quail and cook for an additional 3 minutes.

3) Spread toast with liver spread, place quail on top and serve.

Serves 2

Classic Roasted Quail

8 quails
¾ pound butter
pork fat sheets
3 cups breadcrumbs

1) Coat the quail with butter. Place on a rack in a roasting pan and cover with pork fat. Bake in a preheated 450 degree oven for 25 minutes, basting occasionally with remaining butter. Remove quail and keep warm.

2) Place the breadcrumbs in the pan drippings and brown over a high flame. Split the roasted quail and sprinkle with the browned crumbs.

Serves 4

PHEASANT

Fantastic Pheasant

2 oranges, halved
2 pheasants
½ teaspoon paprika
1 teaspoon rubbed sage
dash of salt
dash of pepper
5 sprigs fresh parsley
5 garlic cloves, peeled
4 tablespoons butter
4 slices bacon
2 cups white wine
1 cup raisins

1) Squeeze the juice from 1 orange inside and outside of the pheasants. Rub with paprika, sage, salt and pepper. Place the parsley, garlic and remaining orange inside the cavity of the pheasant.

2) Coat breast with butter and place in a roasting pan. Place the bacon across the breast, cover with aluminum foil and bake in a preheated 350 degree oven for 45 minutes.

3) Heat wine to boiling, add the raisins and remove from heat. Set aside until pheasant is cooked. Remove the foil around pheasant and spoon the wine and raisins over the bird. Bake uncovered for 45 minutes, basting often.

4) Remove pheasant and spoon sauce on top.

Serves 4

Pheasant with Onion

2 breasts of pheasant, cut in half
6 tablespoons butter
pinch of salt
pinch of pepper
2 onions, quartered
1 cup onion, chopped
2 bay leaves
4 tablespoons flour
3 cups heavy cream
4 tablespoons fresh lemon juice

1) Saute the pheasant in 4 tablespoons butter, salt, pepper, and quartered onion, until brown. Saute chopped onion and bay leaf in remaining melted butter in another pan until onions are transparent.

2) Stir in the flour and cook until it begins to brown. Lower flame, stir in cream and cook for 10 minutes. Strain and mix in the lemon juice. Spoon over the pheasant and serve.

Serves 4

Pheasant Irwin Hill

4 pheasants
1 pound of chestnuts
1½ garlic cloves
⅓ pound butter, melted
4 shallots, minced
1 cup port wine
1 cup mushrooms, sliced
½ teaspoon rosemary
¼ teaspoon thyme
dash of salt
dash of pepper
2 tablespoons lard

1) Boil chestnuts for 15 minutes, let cool and remove the meat. Place garlic in melted butter. Remove garlic and add shallots. Saute over a low flame and add port, mushrooms, chestnuts, rosemary, thyme, salt, and pepper. Mix well.

2) Rub the pheasants with salt and pepper, stuff with the chestnut mixture and close opening. Rub pheasants with butter. Coat two brown paper bags with lard, place the pheasants inside the bags, tie the ends and place in a roasting pan in a preheated 350 degree oven. Cook for 1½ hours.

Serves 4

Pheasant and White Grapes

2 breasts of pheasant, halved
dash of salt
dash of pepper
1 tablespoon butter
2 onions, quartered
1 cup sour cream
1 cup white grapes

1) Lightly season the pheasant with salt and pepper. Add onion and cook in butter until brown.

2) Add sour cream and grapes.

Serves 4

NOTES

NOTES

NOTES

NOTES

NOTES